To Mark.

More than just an
Account Manager

Best wishes
Nick Aldrich
19-9-00.

THE MANY FACES OF
ADMIRAL SIR ROGER CURTIS
*The Story of His Career, Family
and Friendships*

Nicholas Aldrich

NICHOLAS ALDRICH
9 NIGHTINGALE RD
KEMSING KENT

**THE MANY FACES OF
ADMIRAL SIR ROGER CURTIS**
*The Story of His Career, Family
and Friendships*
Copyright © Nicholas Aldrich 1995

All Rights Reserved

ISBN 0-9538836-0-4

First Published June 2000 by

NICHOLAS ALDRICH
9 NIGHTINGALE RD
KEMSING
KENT TN15 6EU

Printed in Great Britain By Unity Print

THE MANY FACES OF
ADMIRAL SIR ROGER CURTIS

*The Story of His Career, Family
and Friendships*

Acknowledgements

It is with great pleasure and gratitude that I express my warm thanks to the many people who have helped me in the production of this dissertation. Firstly, Dr James Thomas and my fellow members of the 'Hampshire' group whose invaluable criticisms have both sharpened and modified this work. For their prompt replies to what were at times very speculative enquiries, I would like to thank the following repositories: The Public Record Office, Portsmouth, City Records Office, the County Records Offices of Hampshire, Wiltshire and Suffolk. The British Library, the National Maritime Museum, the Bank of England, Portsmouth University Library, the Historic Dockyard Chatham, Mr A C Gutridge and Mr Hugh Burns.

Outside of England I am grateful to: The Huntington Library, California and The Boston Public Library, USA and The Brenthurst Library, Johannesburg, South Africa, for their assistance.

Special gratitude goes to Mr Alan King of Portsmouth Central Library and Mr Andrew Trottman of the King Alfred Library, Portsmouth, whose patience in answering my persistent questions and endless visits is appreciated.

For the final draft I would very much like to thank Mary Tunstall who agreed to sort through my rough drafts and type the script. Finally, my heartfelt thanks go to Miss Emma Graveling for persevering and listening so patiently to my ideas at times when her own studies needed attention.

Abstract

Little is known about the career of Admiral Roger Curtis and even less about his family and lifestyle. Yet he was involved in many important naval battles and instrumental in their successful outcome. He commanded many important stations and influenced many of this country's most senior naval officers, such as Lord Howe, Admiral of the Fleet until 1799. At home he gave the impression of a successful and honest family man. Yet, as this study unfolded, evidence (came to light) suggested that Curtis was not all that he seemed. This in turn, raised doubts and questions that whilst in the process of sorting through a wide variety of sources, have shaped the approach taken to this work. Unfortunately, due to the originality of this study and the wide variety of sources that need to be examined, many of these doubts remain unanswered. Each chapter deals with one aspect of Curtis's life, in the hope that (we will know a little more) about the man George III called a 'Naval Hero'.

Abbreviations

C M   -   Court Martial

D.N.B   -   Dictionary of National Biography

G.M.   -   Gentleman's Magazine

N.C.   -   Naval Chronicle

N.R.S.   -   Navy Records Society

P.P.   -   The Portsmouth Papers

V.C.H.   -   Victoria County History

A note on the use of names

When examining the Curtis family, it soon became apparent that many generations of the family used the same christian name Roger. In the interests of continuity, it has been necessary to refer to them by a different title, not just Roger Curtis. Therefore, Sir Roger Curtis will be referred to as either Admiral Curtis, Sir Roger Curtis or just Curtis. Any other member of the family with the name Roger will either be referred to by their full name, e.g. Roger William Curtis, or have the abbreviation (Snr) or (Jnr) next to their name.

List of Tables, Maps, Portraits and Prints

Table of Contents

Introduction

The idea of reconstructing the life and career of one of Britain's Admirals stemmed from a desire to write about the Napoleonic Wars. Suggested to me by my tutor, Dr James Thomas, Sir Roger Curtis presented himself as one of the least written about Admirals of the late eighteenth and early nineteenth centuries. Born to a notable farmer in Downton, Wiltshire, Curtis entered the Navy in 1762 went on to an illustrious career, eventually attained the rank of Admiral of the Red and was created a Baronet.

The approach taken to this study will emphasise many aspects of Curtis's life not just his naval career, as previous studies have done, such as J Ralfe's *The Naval Biography of Great Britain*. Written in 1828, this has been recognised as the most recent biographical study of Admiral Curtis until now. Material for the study was spread far and wide. Much correspondence was sent abroad to repositories such as the Brenhurst Library in South Africa and the Huntington Library in California, an operation involving considerable time and cost. Once obtained, relevant documentation had to be transcribed, an operation producing many valuable and incisive observations concerning the professional and personal life of Curtis.

Professionally, Curtis's use of patronage and friendships with men such as Admiral Lord Howe, resulted in a prominent career in which he reached some of the most senior offices within the Navy. This, however, brought with it criticism from other officers, not all of which was occasioned by personal jealousy. With regard to the patronage, there were further questions which arose. Although asked, however, not all the questions are dealt with owing to a lack of evidence for analysis.

These questions concern the first few months of Curtis's career. How did he obtain his patronage wish such influential men so quickly? This question is complicated by Curtis's lack of naval background, being born a gentleman farmer's son. In *the Dictionary of National Biography*, an answer was proffered by citing a Roger Curtis who served with Sir John Lawson on board the *Swiftsure* 1 in 1662. However, this link is insufficient to account for Curtis's career. What was apparent was that the Curtis name was previously established in farming. For Admiral Curtis, the first member of his family to enter the Navy for a century, no name was established as a seafarer.

Further observations were made concerning the home life of Curtis. In retirement he had amassed a sizeable personal fortune and produced a well respected family. However, probate evidence indicates that there was perhaps a lack of stability within the Curtis household. In a codicil written on 12 November 1816, Curtis revoked all previous provisions for his daughter, Jane, leaving her nothing. Why? Why should he feel compelled to exclude her? Does this suggest a deeper family rift?

Finally, one area which this work will not question, because of constraints of time and space, was the undoubted ability Admiral Curtis had as a Naval Officer. His list of victorious battles was astounding and accounts of his personal courage endless. However, as this study will hopefully prove, it is not always the most able that led this country's Royal Navy. The first question that needs serious consideration then, is what was the nature of his naval career?

Chapter One

Career and Friendships

*Set honour in one eye and death in the other
And I will look on both indifferently:
For, let the Gods so speed me, as I love.
The name of honour more than I fear death.*
Shakespeare. 1

Sir Roger Curtis, the only son of Roger Curtis Esq of Downton near Sailsbury in Wiltshire was born on 4 June 1746 2. An eminent and well respected farmer in that neighbourhood, 3 Roger Curtis, processing considerable wealth and a substantial estate, was a man so much more than his profession suggests. An indication of his stature was the inclusion of his obituary notice in the Gentleman's Magazine for June 1791, the year of his death, in which listed in the obituaries Roger Curtis Esq is to be found. 4 Curtis (sen) had been keen for his only son to follow in his footsteps, to enjoy the ease and independence on his paternal estate. However, his son was set on taking the 'honourable profession': 5 in the Royal Navy. (His father opposed the inclinations of his only son and used every endeavour to dissuade him from the choice he had made). But after using every means possible of parental dissuasion Curtis (sen) resigned himself to his son's choice of career. No evidence has been found to suggest that this upset or damaged their relationship and thus it can be assumed that, all protests being made, they remained good friends.

Curtis entered the Navy in 1762 aged sixteen, on board the *Royal Sovereign* bearing the flag of Vice Admiral Holburne 6. After this he removed to the *Assistance* under Captain J Smith and sailed to the coast of Africa. On his return from Africa he was placed in the *Augusta* (64) at Portsmouth, in which he remained until 1766, when he was ordered to join the *Gibralta* (20) and proceeded to Newfoundland where he served for three years. In 1769 he was received on board the

Venus (36) under the Duke of Cumberland's nominal command, but in reality under that of Captain Barrington (later Admiral Barrington), whom he followed to the Albion 7; and also with whom a close friendship was struck.

During 1771 Curtis was promoted to lieutenant on the *Senegal Sloop* of war, under Captain Morris on the Newfoundland Station. There he had the 'good fortune' to attract the notice of the Governor, Captain (Lord) Shuldham, who having attained his flag, was in 1775 appointed Commander-in-Chief on the North American Station. He took Curtis with him as a lieutenant of the flag ship and in June 1776 promoted him to command the *Senegal* 8. Thus far in Curtis's career it has been his collection of friendships that has helped him gain his promotions, first with Captain Barrington and then with Governor Shuldham. However, it was in the close friendship with Lord Howe as a result of friendship with Shuldham and actions displayed in the American revolt that Curtis's career began to blossom.

In February 1776 Richard Howe was appointed Commander-in-Chief of the North American Station, succeeding Shuldham, who still remained at the station. Howe received this commission jointly with his younger brother, General William Howe, who was already there in command of the Army. 9 With the North American revolt the whole of Howe's command became a scene of obstinate and bloody warfare. For this reason he dispersed his fleets along the coastline, giving younger officers the opportunity to demonstrate their worth. One such officer was Curtis who (according to the Naval Chronical (Vol VI 1801) displayed abilities that might otherwise have remained unnoticed for years. 10 Howe, formed the opinion that there was an able officer. The two were to become good friends , a friendship which was to last until Howe's death in 1799.

It was whilst serving under Howe that Curtis received his next commission in circumstances not normally conducive to promotion. Whilst proceeding to execute the orders given to him by the now Admiral Shuldham, he fell in with a dispersed convoy of transports moving troops to reinforce the army under General W Howe. 11 Conceiving that the safety of the accomplishment of the service on which he was ordered, Curtis collected the convoy and conducted them safely to their place of destination, 12 where he found Lord Howe's flag flying. Called to account for disobeying order, Curtis offered reasons that were so satisfactory to Lord Howe that the latter replied:

I hope I shall never have an officer under my command who has not discretion enough to disobey the orders he may receive from his superiors, when the exigency of the service of his country may require him to do so .... I have much pleasure in presenting you with your commission for the Senegal; Captain Curtis. 13

In this statement Howe demonstrated his confidence in Curtis's ability and the respect he held for him as an officer. Whilst serving as Lord Howe's Captain on the North American Station, Curtis was further promoted to the rank of Post-Captain in 1777 and appointed to command Howe's own ship the *Eagle*. From this period until Lord Howe's death, Curtis served with him wherever his flag was hoisted, except when he commanded the *Brilliant* at Gibraltar. This service together brought with it great friendship and rewards for Curtis's career. (NB when commanding the *Eagle*, Curtis was the youngest Master and Commander in the fleet).14

In 1780 Curtis was given command of the *Brilliant* (28) and ordered to proceed to the Mediterranean. On his arrival in the gut of Gibraltar he was chased by two frigates. After stretching out of his pursuers' reach, however, he arrived safely at Minorca. Here he commenced a series of services connected with Gibraltar's defence and as an aid to his career gained the friendship and respect of General George Eliott, the colony's Governor and a very influential man in naval affairs.

Governor Eliott, finding his provisions running low early in 1781, and being apprehensive that the size of the enemy's fleet might so overmatch the British fleet, formed a plan of sending secretly the *Enterprise*, the *St Fermin Sloop* and the *Fortune* Armed Sloop 15 to join the *Brilliant, Porcupine* and *Minorca Sloop* at Minorca, and there to load all their vessels with provisions and then to force their way into Gibraltar. When his wishes were made known to General Murray and Captain Curtis, the two men went far beyond his warmest expectations. The two officers not only filled the King's vessels, but put a great quantity on board six transports that had remained at Port Mahon ever since the last relief, and also persuaded many private adventurers to accompany them to Gibraltar. Accordingly, Captain Curtis left Port Mahon with 25 sail under convoy and arrived safe at Gibraltar on 27 April 1781. 16 This was only the beginning of many attacks and supply runs made by the British forces and by Captain Curtis in particular. It was these events from 1781 that culminated in his most recognized achievement of this campaign - the events of 13 September 1782.

Early in September 1782 the enemy overpowered one of the British fleet's rendering it necessary to scuttle the ships in the New Mole - this forced the sailors to encamp near Europa Point, forming a land brigade of seamen. Originally, under Eliott's control this brigade was to be commanded by Curtis as a Brigadier. On 13 September 1782 the Spanish executed a vicious and sustained attack upon Gibraltar. The Spanish had also mustered near three hundred large boats to carry troops. The siege had begun. [17]

The battle that followed turned the eyes of Europe towards Gibraltar. The English batteries opened as the enemy came before them and tremendous fire was maintained by both sides. The Spanish floating batteries were supported by cannon and mortar in their lines and approaches. Red-hot shot was sent with such precision from the garrison that smoke was seen from the upper part of the Spanish Admiral's ship. The Spanish attempted to extinguish the fire by the use of fire engines, but their efforts were to prove ineffectual as the fire from the garrison was kept up briskly and that of the enemy gradually decreased. [18] According to contemporary accounts it was during this period that the subsequent actions of Curtis were to be crucial in securing a Spanish withdrawal.

Advancing with the whole division of gun-boats (12), each carrying a twenty-four or eighteen pounder, he formed them so as to flank the line of the enemy's battering ships, while they were harassed by the garrison's heavy and well directed fire. The gun-boats fire was exceedingly well directed , effectually preventing the Spanish from approaching to assist their ships. The Spanish, as a result, fled from their ships, leaving many sailors at the mercy of the English or to the flames of their burning vessels. [19]

These events shows undoubted courage and ability on the part of Curtis, all of which cemented contemporary opinion of him as one of the Navy's finest officers. However, more importantly to the career of Curtis was the manner in which these actions were reported and used by his senior-officers, in this instance by General Eliott and Lord Howe. Writing of these events in his public letter, Eliott observed that:

> *The enemy's daring attempt by sea was effectually defeated by the constant and well supported fire from the batteries; but the well timed judicious and spirited attack made by Brigadier Curtis rendered this success a complete victory.* [20]

In this public address Eliott credited success to Curtis and failed to make reference to any other serving officer. This letter is supported by a further statement given by Howe who arrived in Gibraltar some days later commenting on the bravery of Curtis, which was animated by other British seamen. [21] Writing to Howe, Eliott used the expression: 'if it had not been for his (Captain Curtis) services I will not say the place would have been taken, but I will say it would not have been what it was'. [22] Writing to Curtis in 1797 Lord Howe wrote of Lord Heathfield's comments following the siege of Gibraltar. Heathfield described Curtis as one of this country's most prized national assets. This was high praised indeed for just one man in a campaign that involved hundreds. this letter also shed light on the respect held for Curtis outside of his close relationship between Eliott and Howe. Outside of this professional respect held for Curtis, there is little evidence of his relationship with those he commanded. The only material to be found shedding light upon this was a letter from Admiral Lord Duncan to George Spencer, First Lord of the Admiralty, on 30 June 1797. In this Admiral Duncan conveyed to Spencer his concerns over rumours and complaints from the crew of Roger Curtis's vessel (not named in the letter). This was compounded by Adam's fear that it might led to mutiny. [23] Even though this piece of evidence is not enough to suggest Curtis a poor leader, it does raise questions concerning his character when it came to those he led. Upon Howe's arrival in the flagship the *Victory* that vessel's Captain was quickly dispatched with an account of the fleet's proceedings during the relief of Gibraltar.

A vacancy consequently arose and Curtis was appointed to the *Victory*. However, against Curtis's wishes he was ordered home in the *Thetis* to both give an account of his actions and also to be dubbed. [24] He was subsequently appointed Ambassador to the Emperor of Morocco and the Barbary States, a post which he never filled, being sent back to sea, immediately by Eliott with the rank of Commodore.

In March 1783 Curtis returned to Gibraltar where he remained until the end of that year. In 1784 he was given command of the

Ganges, a guardship in Portsmouth, where he stayed until December 1787. For the next three years he remained in Portsmouth with only light duties, residing at Gatcombe House with his wife and family.

In May 1790 Lord Howe hoisted his flag aboard the *Queen Charlotte* (100) to which Curtis was appointed Captain. After suspected tension arose and died down with Spain during that year, he was appointed to the *Brunswick*, (74) where he remained until 1793. On commencement of the war with France, Howe again intervened in Curtis's career by 'honouring his friend' 25 and making him Captain of the fleet, in which position Curtis returned to the *Queen Charlotte* to assist Howe. During April 1794 Curtis was appointed Colonel of the Plymouth Division of Marines. Shortly after this, he was once more called into action - to take part in the memorable battle of Glorious First of June 1794 under the command of Lord Howe against the French.

At 7.16am on 1 June, Howe signalled that his flag ship was to attack the French centre from there passing through the French line and engaging the enemy from leeward. Following this, each ship was to steer for, and independently engage, her opposite number in the French line. However, unexpectedly the French began a general fire first and as a result the intention of each ship passing astern of her natural opponent did not materialise. Howe, therefore, ordered a general chase. After a brief, but bloody attack, the British had broken the French line, who were now fleeing back towards France. In response, the British gave chase and took six prizes for their efforts as Howe returned to Portsmouth (see chart on British and French lines of Battle).

Howe's fleet returned to Spithead with the six French prizes on 15 June. On 25 June, upon instruction from Howe and the government, the King came to Portsmouth, bringing his Queen and several of his children and awarded chains and medals* to all those officers who had, from Howe's log, distinguished themselves.

Many of the Rear and Vice Admirals received gold chains and medals similar to that given to Lord Howe. Flag Captains received Medals - at least a certain number of them did. Only one Captain received a medal and chain - Roger Curtis. The award to Curtis was given to him on Howe's instruction of his services as Captain of the flagship. The lack of reward for other officers resulted in a wave of ill-feeling by those who felt their actions as equally deserving. From this episode an examination of the response by Curtis to this professional jealousy reveals further questions concerning his character. This exclusion upset and annoyed, in particular, Captain Cuthbert Collingwood, serving on the *Barfluer* whose senior officer, Rear Admiral Gardner was rewarded. In correspondence with Edward Blackett Collingwood knew exactly who was to blame for this snub. (These medals are regarded as the first Naval Medals issued). After conveying to Blackett his actions and subsequent lack of reward, Collingwood commented on a letter sent by Howe which gave for his Medal choices:

> *Lord Howe is less blamed for his letter than his Captain, who ever has been artful, sneaking creature, whose fawning insinuating manners creeps into the confidence of whoever he attacks, and whose rapacity would grasp all honours and all profits that come within his view. The letter was an attempt upon the credulity of the world to make them believe the Queen Charlotte with very little help defeated the French fleet. It may be considered as a libel on the fleet.* 26

When Collingwood received the letter from Howe listing those to receive medals and an account of the events, he went to see Howe immediately. 27 However, he got no further than his secretary, Sir R C or as Collingwood referred to him 'fabricator' of his letter 28 Collingwood, already angry at being denied access to Howe, told Curtis.

> *I consider, Sir Roger, that the conduct of the Barfleur merited commendation when commendation was given to zeal and activity. This insinuation that either was wanting is injurious and unjust. No ship was more than warmly or effectively engaged than the Barfleur from the beginning to the end of the action. And (he added sarcastically); it was not our fault that the Frenchmen did not knock our mast array.* 29

This accusation was rebutted by Curtis who demonstrated to Collingwood that this exclusion was not a slur against his skill or exertion. 30 This raises questions as to why Sir Roger did not defend the choices made by Howe, suggesting perhaps a weakness in Curtis's character - a desire to shy away from personal confrontation. Added to the grievances of Collingwood were those of Schomberg of the *Culloden;* Bazeley of the *Alfred* and Elphinstone of the *Glory*, all angered at their omission from the medal list and who all felt that Curtis had a hand in this. By blaming Curtis it suggests that Sir Roger's patronage with Howe was viewed with jealousy by other officers. It is difficult to gauge the influence Curtis held over Howe's decision making. However, the possible explanation for this lay, not in Howe's weakness, but in the special friendship between the two men. From this friendship it is no coincidence that on 4 July 1794 Roger Curtis was promoted to Rear Admiral of the *Blue* and created a baronet, again upon Howe's recommendation. Further elements to Curtis's character were touched upon in a letter between Collingwood and Blackett, in which the former made reference to what he considered to be the main purpose of Sir Roger's career - 'To grasp all honour and all profits'. Again perhaps motivated by jealousy, Collingwood suggested that Curtis was centred in his acquisition of the most lucrative prizes at whatever cost. Admiral Murray writing to Admiral Markham commented that when Curtis declined to engage the enemy in battle he still requested the majority share of all the prizes taken. In this respect Murray felt that Sir Roger's only purpose was 'To have taken what he could and gone away with the booty'. 31 This impression of Curtis is confirmed in a letter by him to John Spencer, First Lord of the Admiralty. In this Curtis complained of the lack of pickings on his station, the Isle De France and requested that this merited being transferred to where prizes were abundant. 32 One month later, on 26 February 1799, Curtis was appointed Commander-in-Chief of the Cape. 33

This is not to suggest that this was the only reason for the appointment. Curtis had proved his ability on numerous occasions. Indeed, following the 1 June 1795 action, Sir Roger was regarded as a national hero. However, the sudden vacancy of the post in the Cape so soon after this personal request does raise questions as to what or who, was the motivating force for this appointment. Here was the clearest indication of the influence Curtis held under Howe's patronage. The only question that remains in this case was whether this transfer was as a result of pressure by Howe or Curtis's friendship with Spencer?

On 5 August 1799 Lord Howe died after receiving electricity as a treatment for gout. ₃₄ This came as a severe blow to Curtis both personally and professionally, who by now was seeking to further the careers of his sons, Roger and Lucius. To this end, he had by now established a firm friendship with Lord St Vincent, Howe's replacement and in so doing, helped to secure promotions for his sons. This change in loyalty did not show that Curtis's friendship with Howe was superficial. What it did point to was Sir Roger's professionalism and realisation of the ways in which the Navy operated.

As mentioned above in 1799 Curtis was appointed Commander-in-Chief of the Cape where he remained for four years. In April 1804 he was promoted to Admiral of the *Blue*. Between 1805 and 1808 he was instructed to take up office as one of the Commissioners for revising the Civil Affairs and King's Regulations of the Navy. Admiral Curtis's main contribution to the Regulations was an article drawn up with Admiral Lord Gambier in which the long established order for ships of war to compel all foreign ships to salute the King's flag within the narrow seas should be omitted. ₃₅ In January 1809 he was appointed Commander-in-Chief at Portsmouth, where he served the full term of five and a half years. In 1815 Sir Roger was created a Knight Grand Cross, his final reward which he took to retirement. Curtis was an officer of undoubted ability, courage and fortitude. Throughout he distinguished himself in battle many times, most notably in Gibraltar where his presence of mind saved the colony from falling into Spanish hands, as has been indicated, ability alone cannot account for his rise through the ranks. It was a collection of influential friendships and Howe's patronage in particular that Curtis used to secure promotion. From the evidence presented Curtis was ambitious and cunning, knowing exactly what he wanted.

Little evidence survives to support suggestions of friendship and influence, but what evidence there is did highlight further explanations for his advancement. However, this alone cannot account for his rise. His undoubted ability as a naval officer earnt him praise on numerous occasions and established his position. (The point this chapter is arguing is just that). There were many other skilled and courageous naval officers, such as Collingwood and Bazeley, who did not rise so rapidly and who only did so following changes in the Admiralty. Why was it Curtis shone out above the others? Was it through his patrons or was it through less obvious doorways, such as a sycophantic following of Howe?

Chapter Two

Curtis and Portsmouth

In January 1809 Admiral Sir Roger Curtis was appointed Commander-in-Chief of His Majesty's Ships and Vessels at Spithead and in Portsmouth Harbour by the Board of the Admiralty replacing Admiral Montagu and beating Lord Leith and Sir Charles Cotton to the post. It was an office in which he possessed all the rights, honours and responsibilities from the date on which his flag was hoisted until it was finally haulted down. 1

From the time of Henry VIII Portsmouth has been the pride of the British Navy. 2 It was for this reason that the office to which Curtis was appointed was keenly observed and influenced by the Lords of the Admiralty and perhaps, therefore, the tasks that were undertaken with the office were considerably more important and more sought after than those of Commander-in-Chief of other stations. Curtis had many duties as Commander-in-Chief. Some included: causing the ships of his fleet or Squadron, manned and armed, to be frequently assembled, inspected and exercised in manoeuvres in landing, embarking and boarding vessels. He would see that the vessels of his Fleet were frequently practised in exercises in port and in performing manoeuvres at sea. He was also responsible for frequent exercising the officers in making night-and-day signals to ensure accuracy. In the event of visiting foreign officials to Portsmouth, he would act as the Crown's diplomatic representative and would be expected to entertain and accommodate them in Portsmouth. The Commander-in-Chief of Portsmouth being frequently invested with great charge, on which the fate of the nation may depend must possess the abilities equal to so important a station and so extensive a command. His Fleet was unavoidably exposed to a variety of perplexing situations. The health, order and discipline of his men were no less the objects of his consideration than the condition and quality of ships. His skill could be employed to counteract the various disasters which his Fleet may suffer from different causes. His vigilance and presence of mind were necessary to seize every favourable opportunity that his situation may offer to prosecute his principle designs, to extricate himself from any difficulty or distress; to check unfortunate events in the beginning and retard the progress of any great calamity. Sir Roger Curtis should be embued with resolution and fortitude to animate his officers by force of example and promote a sense of emulation. Curtis was also instructed by the Admiralty to ensure safe passage through his waters for Merchant shipping. To this end, he would order surveys to be made of all the dangers to navigation within the Portsmouth waters. Furthermore, in a time of war he would afford convoy and protection to the Merchantmen of Great Britain and her allies. The most essential part of his duty, however, was military conduct. He was required to keep pace with the various improvements in vessels and ordnance and changes in the Fleet tactics. When preparing a Fleet or Squadron for sea in time of war, as the vessels join him, he was to furnish each commanding officer with a copy of all general orders, dispositions, private signals and orders of battle so that they would understand what their responsibilities were when going into battle. [3] Finally he was expected to be well versed with the principles of international and naval law, so that he could judge with propriety the proceedings of Courts Martial and correct the errors and restrain the abuses, which may happen therein by mistake, ignorance or inattention. It was whilst conducting this responsibility that Curtis presided over the Court Martial of Admiral James Lord Gambier, a Court Martial in which Curtis perhaps abused the power of the office which has previously been described.

On 26 July 1809 a Court Martial was assembled on board His Majesty's Ship *Gladiator* in Portsmouth harbour. The charge was read against Lord Gambier:

> *That Admiral the Right Honourable Lord Gambier on the 12th April, the enemy's ships being then on shore, and the signal having been made that they could be destroyed, did for a considerable time, neglect or delay taking effectual measures for destroying them.* [4]

James Gambier, created Lord Gambier on 9 November 1807.

Admiralty Commission March 1795 to February 1801;
May 1804 - February 1804; April 1807 to May 1808.

Source: Portraits and Prints Catalogue: National Maritime Museum
(nd).

The Court Martial against Gambier was called by the Admiralty in response to Gambier's personal request, that he be Court Martialled in an attempt to clear his name concerning accusations made by Captain Thomas (Lord) Cochrane surrounding the events of April 1809 in the Basque and Axis Road waters off the French coast.

Gambier (1756-1833) (see portrait on previous page) was an officer with an unquestionable ability and an unblemished service record.   Entering the navy at (the age of) eleven, Gambier (soon) progressed through the ranks, attaining the rank of Lieutenant on 12 February 1777 at 21.   After a successful command on the North American Station, he returned to England to command HMS *Defence* for service in the Channel against the French (1794). It was whilst in action on board the *Defence* on 1st June 1794 that Gambier distinguished himself in battle by breaking through the French line of defence.   For this he received a Gold Medal from close personal friend, Lord Howe, Admiral of the Channel Fleet. In 1799 Gambier was promoted to Vice-Admiral and in 1802 was appointed Governor and Commander-in-Chief of Newfoundland.

Upon his return in 1807 Gambier was appointed as a Sea Lord to the Admiralty whereupon he worked and socialised very closely with Curtis. 5 Together they revised *the King's Regulations and Admiralty Instructions*.   From this Gambier extended his circle of friends to encompass Lord Howe (and other Sea Lords) and Curtis in particular who, by 1806, held great influence in Naval affairs.

In July 1807 Gambier became an Admiral and was given the command of the Prince of Wales and the Channel Fleet where he proceeded to the Baltic to launch an attack against the Danish. 6 Gambier triumphed and returned to England with the Danish Navy in tow.   For this he was hailed a hero both by the public and perhaps more importantly, by the politicians and for this action was raised to the peerage. His next naval encounter of note would be the Basque and Axis Roads campaign in March and April 1809.   Throughout his career Gambier had always been a very strict Methodist, known for his charitable work and favouring traditional naval practices, especially in time of war concerning strategy and method. This was a belief which he carried with him to the Basque and Axis Roads, but one which conflicted sharply with those of Captain Thomas (Lord) Cochrane.

Thomas (Lord) Cochrane (1775-1860) 10th Earl of Dundonald,
Admiral.

Source: Portrait and Prints Catalogue: National Maritime Museum
(nd).

Cochrane (1775-1869) (see picture on previous page) was the 10th Earl of Dundonald who, unlike Gambier, had joined the navy at the comparatively mature age of seventeen and a half. In 1795 he was made Lieutenant of the *Thetis* and accompanied Lord Keith 7 to North America and the Mediterranean, which considering at the age of twenty, after only two and a half years service, was a considerable responsibility. This upset many older and established officers. Thomas Cochrane was a very practical naval officer distinguishing himself in battle many times. Of note were his actions in the Blockade of Cadiz in 1799-1800, where he was credited as heroic in HMS *Barfleur*. However, Cochrane also possessed a very violent temper, a temper for which he was reprimanded on many occasions, especially with a First Lieutenant by the name of Philip Beaver who brought Cochrane to a Court Martial for disrespect. Cochrane's good friend Lord Keith secured Cochrane's acquittal. 8 By now, however, Cochrane was making powerful enemies at the Admiralty. It would be wrong, however, to misjudge Cochrane's ability as a naval officer. Although his methods were unconventional, his success rate was high. In one incident, knowing the Spanish were following his ship, he disguised his vessel in Danish colours and dressed himself and his crew in Danish uniforms. When a Spanish Frigate ran up close to him he hoisted the quarantine flag, so the Spanish left them alone and sailed past. 9 This story may not be the truth, after all, it is doubtful whether naval practice was to carry the uniforms of your enemy, but it does suggest Cochrane's ingenuity and character. He was an officer who did not conduct his affairs by the rule book, but who achieved a high level of success.

In 1807 Cochrane was elected for Westminster. It was in this capacity that he brought forward a motion on the naval abuses of Admiralty power. This action by Cochrane does seem rather bizarre on the understanding that a serving naval officer should publicly question the power held by the Admiralty; but this action is not surprising of an officer who never followed tradition.

Captain Cochrane's first encounter with Gambier came about as a result of an Admiralty enquiry into the use of Fire Ships. 10 In the campaign in the Bay of Biscay led by Gambier in February 1809. 11 Lord Gambier wrote 'That though the enemy's ships may lie much exposed to the operation of fire ships, it is a horrible mode of warfare and the attempt hazardous if not desperate'. 12 Cochrane asked by the Admiralty for an opinion of this, advocated the use of fire ships. On this point the Admiralty agreed with him. Cochrane added to his comments that:

> *He represented that being a junior officer, his doing so would excite a great deal of jealousy. That Lord Gambier might consider it presumptuous and might not impossibly deem the plan still more desperate and horrible than that to which he had already objected.* 13

To this comment Lord Mulgrave 14 eased his fears by saying he would so manage it with Lord Gambier, but no attempt to allay this jealousy was made and Cochrane on his arrival to the Channel Fleet found himself exposed to the indignation of every officer senior to himself. Gambier virtually refused to have anything to do with Cochrane, while Admiral Harvey told Cochrane that as he himself had volunteered for that service in the Bay of Biscay, he could only consider his being specially sent out as an insult to the Channel Fleet. 15 The Admiralty ordered Gambier to destroy the French Fleet. Gambier responded that he would do all that is possible to achieve this matter what the consequence to crew or vessels. 16

On the night of 11 April 1809 Cochrane had positioned his Fire Ships and Explosion vessels (which he was given command of perhaps as a gesture to his remarks in the Bay of Biscay) behind the Isle Madame (see map). On the other side of the Island on the mainland positioned between Chateau Le Foires and Fort De La Pointe, the French Fleet had ran aground as the tide had gone out. Aware of this Cochrane signalled to Gambier at 5.48am for permission to attack. After a lengthy delay and many signals (see appendix no...) Gambier responded at 9.30am, issuing the order. By now, many French ships had begun to float as the tide was rising. As a result of this delay, Cochrane was faced with a bloody battle in which his command was vastly outnumbered. At 1.45pm Cochrane requested help from the Channel Fleet, at that time fourteen miles away.

18

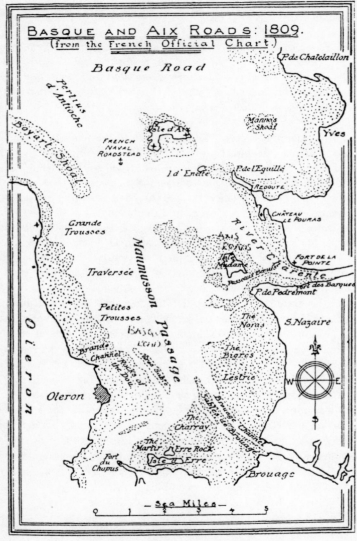

Source: W Laid-Clowes; The Royal Navy - A History Volumes 1897 - 1903, Vol V, 1900, p260.

Signals from Cochrane to Gambier

Table

At 5.48am 'Half the fleet can destroy the enemy, seven on shore.

At 6.40am 'Eleven on shore'.

At 7.40am 'Only two afloat'.

At 9.30am 'Enemy preparing to heave off'.

It was only on the last of these signals that Gambier decided to attack - this was the result:

At 1.30pm   'The enemy's ships are getting under sail'.

At 1.40pm   'The enemy is superior to the chasing ship'.

At 1.45pm   'The ship is in distress and requires to be assisted immediately'.

Source: W Laird-Clowes, *The Royal Navy, A History* (VII Volumes 1897-1903, Vol V, (1900), p 264.

When Gambier on board the *Imperieuse* and the Fleet eventually arrived, Cochrane's command was severely depleted, but had managed with further help from Gambier to destroy a vast number of French ships. Cochrane then requested further permission to chase the now fleeing French Fleet up the river Charents; Gambier denied this request and ordered the Fleet home. Upon returning to Portsmouth, Gambier and Cochrane were welcomed as heroes. The Times spoke of their courageous bravery 17 and the Chancellor of the Exchequer concluded a speech, in which he highly eulogized Gambier's conduct by proposing a parliamentary vote of thanks. However, this vote of thanks was opposed by Thomas Cochrane and Sir Francis Burdett, a close friend of Cochrane. Gambier, upon hearing the news of this slur against his character requested that the Admiralty conveve a Court Martial so that an official investigation could be launched into his conduct as commanding officer in the Basque and Axis Roads in March and April 1809.

Unwilling to conduct this Court Martial, the Admiralty attempted to persuade Gambier against such proceedings. For Gambier, however, it was his honour that was at stake. The Admiralty, unable to change Gambier's mind, contacted Sir Roger Curtis, a close personal friend and instructed him to conduct a 'friendly court' 18 in this case. Cochrane on 29 May 1809 was ordered to prefer his charges which he declined doing, answering that the log and signal log books of the Fleet contained all particulars and furnished premises whence accurate conclusions might be drawn. 19 He thus had to bear all the odium of having accused his Commander-in-Chief, without the compensating advantage of being in a position to prove his accusations. The Court Martial was convened on 26 July 1809 and lasted none days. During this time it seems questionable as to who was on trial - Gambier or Cochrane. Sir Roger Curtis was well versed in Law, it being after all, one of his responsibilities as Commander-in-Chief and these legal skills were shown to their fullest in this trial.

The case for the defence, as with the prosecution centred around the log and signal log book. For the prosecution Charles Bicknell, Prosecutor for the Navy attempted to show that the log and signal log book clearly stated the time of the signals from Cochrane to Gambier, with the delays in responding and also the refusal to issue the order to pursue the French, thus showing gross neglect of command. The defence, presented by Gambier, attempted to ascertain the logs authenticity on the understanding that because Cochrane had written the logs post the event, indeed being written after the Court Martial had been called, that they were an invalid source of evidence and perhaps not even the truth. Lord Gambier attempted to prove that

Lord Cochrane had falsified the logs to support the prosecution. [20] After this opening address was presented by both parties, it is interesting to see the pattern of investigation taken by Sir Roger Curtis as President of the Court Martial. From studying the minutes of the Court Martial it seems as though his questions centred around the falsifying of the logs. It is unclear whether this was an instruction from the Admiralty or whether Curtis used friendship to decide upon his line of questioning. [21] What is clear, however, is that it seems as though Cochrane was on trial not Gambier. Curtis went on to use prosecution as well as defence questioning to suite Gambier. Curtis disallowed the notes written by Cochrane post the event as evidence and at all times throughout the hearing reiterated the disgrace Cochrane had brought upon the Navy by questioning Admiral Gambier's honour.

Gambier's defence rested upon proving his actions as justifiable and to discredit the prosecutions case. To begin with Gambier questioned the reliability of the logs kept by Cochrane claiming they were falsified by Cochrane. He then went on to explain the reasons for his actions; some of these included: The safety of the crews, wrong position of the tide in the Channel; that signals sent by Cochrane were responded to after adequate consideration. Gambier also remonstrated that he saw the need to preserve and return the vessels under his charge. [22] Furthermore, he considered that as action was a success, there was no need to pursue the French beyond the Basque and Axis Roads. However, points relating to the safety of the crew and the preservation of the vessels directly contradicted a letter sent by Gambier to W W Pole on 26 March 1809 [23], in which he had stated, 'I am ready to obey any order they may be pleased to honour me with, *however*, great risk may be to the loss of men and ships'. [24] The subsequent order from the Admiralty was to destroy the entire French Fleet. Therefore, could Gambier have disobeyed the orders? On Friday 4 August 1809 the ninth day, both parties were asked to sum up. Gambier presented first, followed by Cochrane, who used this time to convey a personal letter to Curtis. In this letter Cochrane stated that 'Having learnt from my fellow brother officers' [25] that rumours had been 'sent abroad' that Cochrane had censored the conduct of other officers involved in these events, he wanted the Court to acknowledge that this was untrue. The Court did not acknowledge this, Curtis merely agreeing to enter this letter into the minutes.

Therefore, not only had the navy, no doubt, spread this rumour, but by Curtis's command this rumour was not officially stopped.

The verdict of the Court was thus:

> *'That the charge has not been proved against the said Admiral, the Right Honourable Lord, but this his Lordships conduct and proceedings as Commander-in-Chief of the Channel Fleet employed in the Basque Roads between 17 March and 29 April, was marked by ZEAL, JUDGEMENT, ABILITY and an anxious attention to the welfare of His Majesty's service and both adjudge him to be most honourably acquitted'.* 26

Following this Curtis returned Gambier's sword and said:

> *'Having so far obeyed the command of this Court, I beg you will permit me, in my individual capacity to express to you the high gratification I have upon this occasion'.* 27

By using the word 'individual', Curtis displayed a preference for Gambier. This is not a comment on behalf of the navy, but on behalf of himself. Curtis was pleased that Gambier had been acquitted. From this it is possible to begin to realise the friendship between these two men, as well as giving a further insight into the character of Sir Roger Curtis. From the manner in which the questioning was conducted, it became apparent where preference lay. However, it is only with this final comment by Curtis that it becomes clear that it is through personal opinion rather than from Admiralty orders, of which none can be found, that this summary is based upon.

As a consequence of this Court Martial, Gambier was re-appointed Commander-in-Chief of the Channel Fleet and re-affirmed friendships with Curtis. For Cochrane, his immediate career was ruined, being suspended from the Navy and through an unproven Stock Market scandal lost his seat as an MP. It was only after the current Admiralty Board that changed all its members that Cochrane was re-appointed to the Navy whereupon he attained the rank of Admiral. 28

This individual case study into the service record of Sir Roger Curtis as Commander-in-Chief of Portsmouth leaves many unanswered questions about the events and the relationships shared by the three men. Was the Court Martial a mere charade to disgrace Captain Cochrane? Whose recollection of the events was the truth? Was it too dangerous to pursue the French? Was there such a level of jealousy between Gambier and Cochrane that it should lead to this? Was there such a great level of social and professional antagonism between these two officers of undoubted ability? Finally, to what extent did the friendship between Curtis and Gambier influence the trial's outcome?

It is these questions that, given more time, need to be developed to give a greater understanding of the events of March and April 1809.

To what extent did this Court Martial reflect upon the character and ability of Sir Roger Curtis as Commander-in-Chief? Correspondence and diaries can be used to assess Curtis's character as well as his abilities.

Admiral Curtis was seen throughout his time as Commander-in-Chief, as a very honourable man, who though favouring tradition, did not stop progress. As commanding officer he was trusted and respected by the Admiralty and his fellow officers and ratings. In correspondence from Curtis to Admiral Markham, Curtis expressed his gratitude for the sympathy shown to his family upon his son's (Roger) death. This letter highlighted the respect Markham held for the Curtis family and gave indications of the sensitive nature of Curtis in responding to this with a letter showing genuine appreciation, to a lower ranked officer. 29

As mentioned previously, Curtis was an honourable Commander-in-Chief who respected the institutions of the Navy. This was particularly highlighted in Lord Gambier's Court Martial.

Although the case presented in this chapter may suggest that friendship was the greatest piece of evidence, this is not to suggest that Curtis was corrupt. Both Gambier's and the Navy's honour was brought into question by Cochrane. Curtis was disgusted that such a young officer with a cavalier naval record should question naval traditions, not only in this case, but in Cochrane's position as an MP, where he questioned the Admiralty's role. Thus, the picture that emerges to date of Curtis as Commander-in-Chief is one of a caring, traditional and honourable man.

To this can be added Curtis's comical or light-hearted side. In a series of recollections by James Anthony Garner (Commander, RN, 1775-1814). Gardner recalled the time Curtis complimented a young Midshipman called Mr Stevens, for being the first to go aloft when the order was given to loosen the mizen sail of a vessel anchored in Portsmouth Harbour, 'You are a fine fellow, Mr Stevens; a most active officer, Mr Stevens; you a wonder Mr Stevens'. 30 It, unfortunately happened that Mr Stevens was left behind by the other Midshipman and was in fact last on the yard. Sir Roger Curtis when being told of this called out, 'I recall all my compliments Mr Stevens; you are a dammed lubber Mr Stevens; a blockhead Mr Stevens; come down Mr Stevens'. 31 To complete this picture of Sir Roger Curtis as Commander-in-Chief, all that is needed is an example of his dedication to his duties. Evidence for this can be found in the letter previously mentioned to Captain Markham. In the final paragraph, Curtis made reference to a request to Lord St Vincent, Sea Lord to the Admiralty, to be returned to active duty. From this it can be ascertained that Curtis was given compassionate leave for his son in July 1801. In this case the loss of his son was great, but Curtis considered his responsibilities to Portsmouth as important being stationed to the guardship *Ganges*, especially as this was during the Napoleonic Wars, and as such Curtis held a vital position in the defence of England.

Even though the example was not as Commander-in-Chief, Curtis still proved a very worthy Commander-in-Chief and held the office without fault for the full term (five and a half years). However, the final comment as to the effectiveness, ability and character of Sir Roger Curtis as Commander-in-Chief must come from those who appointed him to the Admiralty. This can be found in a letter from Admiralty Secretary York to Curtis:

> *'It is almost superfluous for me to endeavour to express the perfect satisfaction I have experienced during the time I have presided at the Admiralty, in the zealous correct and able assistance, which has been derived to the public service from your intendence at Portsmouth. Had I remained at the Board, I should have felt extremely uneasy at finding a successor for your command and I cannot omit taking this opportunity of expressing my high sense of the very able manner in which you have uniformly fulfilled the duties on your important stations.'* 32

Chapter Three

Family and Lifestyle

On the right of the London Road near Hilsea is Gatcombe House, the seat of the gallant Admiral Sir Roger Curtis. A vista remarkable for its simplicity and dignity opens the view of the villa, which is a respectable mansion situated where tranquillity invites you to enjoy all her charms of heart-soothing retirement.

The distance from the road is sufficient to afford a sight of passing society without being disturbed by the rude clamour of whirling carriages, horses, etc. or offend with the clouds of dust raised in dry weather by coaches, chaises, carts, wagons, etc. in all roads so incessantly frequented as that between Portsmouth and London. 1

Admiral Curtis's association with Portsmouth began long before his time as Commander-in-Chief in 1809. On 12 December 1778 he married Sarah Brady, daughter of Matteate Brady, a wealthy ex-army officer in the parish of Saint Mary's Portsea. Brady owned Gatcombe House, the large manorial seat of Gatcombe Manor, Portsmouth. It was bounded on the south by Stubbington Avenue and on the east and west by Copnor and London Roads respectively. 2 *The Hampshire Telegraph* for 3 June 1833 described it as consisting of numerous rooms of good proportions, well fitted up and replete with fixtures, good underground wine and beer cellars, large kitchen, servants hall and other offices. Outside of the house there was a double coach house, which consisted of an excellent five stall stable with harness rooms and lofts above; a large greenhouse on the lawn of upwards of an acre and this was surrounded by two kitchen gardens. Leading up to the house there was a six acre walk meadow. 3 Matteate Brady gave the house (see opposite) and all its lands to the newly wed couple as a wedding gift and from then on Gatcombe House became the Curtis family seat. What Sarah Brady's elder sister, Jane thought

The current Gatcombe House was built in 1870 on a site that has been in use since the 12 century when the priory Church of Gatcombe had occupied the land.

Source: P Rogers, Cosham with Widley and Hilsea in old picture postcards, (European Library) 1986 picture 102.

of this gift remains a mystery for the present, for at the time of the wedding she was residing in Gatcombe House. From the wedding her whereabouts remain unknown and it is not impossible that soon after she too married and moved on.

Curtis and his wife had two sons and a daughter. The first son and eldest child was named Roger after his father. He and the second son Lucius born 3 June 1786 both followed in their father's footsteps and joined the Navy. The other child was a daughter Jane, of whom little evidence has come to light to date. Roger Curtis (jun) was the first to enter the Navy and with help from his father, who had on occasion petitioned both Lord Howe and the Earl St Vincent, had reached the rank of Post-Captain by early 1801. It was during this year that he was posted to the Cape to take command of the *Rattlesnake*. Upon his in 1802 Roger Curtis (jun) succumbed to an illness on 12 July of that year at Bristol Hotwells. Little is known about the disease which struck him down, beyond that it was a painful disorder which baffled all medical skill. 4 His death was to hit the Curtis family very hard. His mother took it the hardest and she was herself struck with an illness not physical, but one from which, so Sir Roger Curtis informed Admiral Markham, she would never recover. The death also affected Admiral Curtis, who as a result, was given indefinite shore leave. This, however, only lasted three months as he was keen to return to service. 5 Their second son Lucius was to be more fortunate, embarking on a glowing naval career which culminated in his attaining the rank of Admiral of the Fleet. He married Mary Figg, eldest daughter of Moses Greetham of East Cosham, a former Deputy Judge Advocate of the Fleet on 1 June 1811. Together they had four sons and three daughters. The eldest two sons, both called Roger, (the first was born 9 November 1812, the second 8 May 1816) also entered the Navy and went on to have successful careers. However, it was the influence of Sir Roger Curtis, which proved to be the key in Lucius's rise to the top for the Admiral became his son's patron. Lucius entered the Navy on 2 June 1795 as Captain's Servant on board the *Queen Charlotte* bearing his father's flag. Sir Roger Curtis introduced Lucius to Lord Howe, who secured a commission for him on board the *Royal William* as Lieutenant, eighteen months after entering the Navy. 6 This method of promotion was not uncommon for this period, in fact it was common naval practice. But it does go in part to prove that it was not always the most able officers which achieved success.

As well as his career in the Navy, Lucius Curtis had a keen interest in local affairs and establishing his own estate. Lucius was a County Magistrate [7] and thanks to donations of land from his father in Suffolk, Wiltshire and Hampshire owned a sizeable estate. His principle home was Ramsbridge Cottage near Weyhill. This was a splendid house set in 116 acres of Parkland. Ramsbridge had for many centuries been the manorial seat for Weyhill. It had also housed many years previous, royalty, with both Edward II and Richard I using it as their hunting retreat. However, at that time it was known as Ramsbridge House. [8] Sir Lucius also hunted from here and became a prominent figure building himself a strong reputation as a hunter. Lucius hunted with his pack of harriers in the lands around Andover and Chilbolten. [9] However, on occasions these harriers brought jealousy and frustration from other huntsmen who envied his pack and success:

> *It was with these hounds that Mr Asseheton Smith was so much annoyed and he is said to have done all he could to persuade Sir Lucius to part with his pack and leave off hunting the district. On one occasion he is reported to have said to the owner of the pack; if you will give up your harriers, I will make you a present of the best hunter that many can buy.* [10]

Lucius, like his father, was a keen collector of naval literature, although no accounts of his collection could be found from the Will of Curtis, bequeathing his collection to his son Lucius, it became apparent that Admiral Curtis's love for books on navigation and combat strategy was shared by his son. Curtis's youngest child Jane, seems to have been forgotten in a family so well connected with naval life. In Admiral Curtis's Will some clues are given as to her situation. By 1816 she appears to have been unmarried, but from an entry to the Will on 26 July 1816, to have had a daughter. Unfortunately, no evidence could be found to elaborate upon this, but as well be shown later, this child was to prove the stumbling block in the relationship between father and daughter.

The Curtis Family

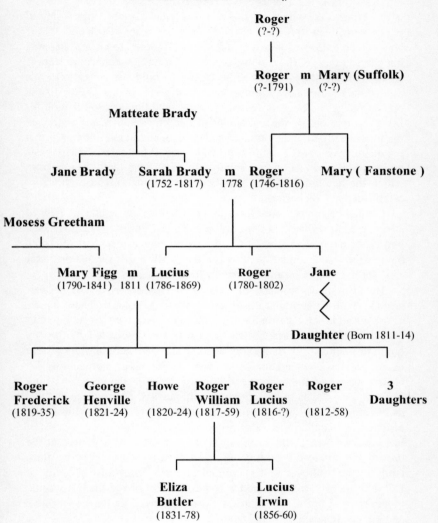

Source: Catherington Church, MIs; various sources for which see footnotes.

From his seat at Gatcombe House, Admiral Curtis enjoyed many other pastimes, not just keeping abreast of current developments in naval affairs, of which he possessed a considerable library, all of which was given to his son at the time of the death. Sir Roger Curtis was a keen collector of wines and spirits. Indeed, so consuming was his passion that by the time of his death he had extended the storage space of his cellars at Gatcombe House to hold his collection. An indication of the sheer volume kept was given in his Will. In the opening pages he bequeathed all his wines and liqueurs to his wife for her consumption for the remainder of her life. And if any remained upon her death, then the remainder should go to Lucius. To imply that the quantity was sufficient to last for the rest of his wife's life suggests an impressive collection or a sober wife. The most likely source from which the alcohol had been supplied was Arthur Purchase and Son, established at Chichester.11

Gardening, music, horses and collectables particularly plated silver were the main hobbies of Sir Roger Curtis. He possessed numerous musical instruments and musical manuscripts, all of which he held very dear to him, leaving originally all of them to his daughter Jane for her to cherish and preserve within the family.

He also made full use of Gatcombe House's five-stall stables, within which he kept and cared for his carriage horses. These horses along with his three carriages, gigs and harnesses were to be given to his wife until her death. Then they were to be sold, all the money going to Lucius. The remaining horses were to be kept until they were of no good use, whereupon they were to be killed humanely. By clearly listing as one of the conditions of the Will, the humane killing of the horses Curtis indicated the importance and devotion he showed to his animals. In addition to the livestock at Gatcombe House, the grounds surrounding were also impressive; consisting of eight acres of lawn and kitchen gardens and an attached farm. Even though at the turn of the nineteenth century he was forced to sell most of his farm land to the military under compulsory purchase for the sum of £24,000. 12 He still retained a reduced farm and gardens. Curtis, however, was not a keen gardener and employed gardeners, farmers and kitchen hands to tend his land.

As a man of substantial wealth and title, Admiral Curtis furnished his home lavishly. He owned a large collection of paintings, one being a gift from Lord and Lady Howe, the Rysdale. 13 He subscribed to many books including J S Clark & J Miaither, *The Life of Admiral*

Lord Nelson (1809) and *The British Flag Triumphant* (1806) in order to stock his considerable library. He also amassed many jewels, rings, watches, trinkets and wearing apparel, all of which went to underline his standing within Portsmouth society. He possessed a considerable collection of plate and plated articles which were to be singled out for special mention in his estate. In his Will he was most implicit in his request that these were to be given to Lucius for him to use and subsequently to pass on. Along with the Rysdale from Lord Howe, these possessions were never to be sold.

An important part of Curtis's life was his provisions for the future, his investments. He opened several bank accounts both personal and naval. However, it is his accounts with the Bank of England that are of particular interest. He held three accounts with the Bank in all - a Navy Stock account with his holding by 1797 being 5% a personal account in 3% Consols, opening in July 1784 with £3,500 and a joint account with Sir John Carter and Sir John Godwin, opening in February 1794 with £1,150 and closing in September 1810 with the same account. 14

Admiral Curtis's personal account highlighted his keen eye for investment and securing his financial position. His account records show many entries of substantial sums by W Marriott, some single entries totalling in excess of £3,500. Marriott was a London-based Stockbroker who operated on behalf of Sir Roger Curtis's holdings in shares and bonds and from all accounts conducted his job successfully. Evidence for this came in the balance of the account at the time of Admiral Curtis's death. While the opening balance was £3,500 the balance on 14 November 1816 was £67,431 (by the Bank of England's calculation as of October 1994, this figure is equivalent to over three quarters of a million pounds, in one account). 15

This account was left open long after Curtis's death and where the money's raised from the sale and leasing of his estate were placed. His account was operated by his three executors: Sir Lucius Curtis, William Eley Cook of the *Adelphi* and Thomas Andrews Minchin of the Grove, Alverstone, Hampshire. This practice was not uncommon for this period, indeed it was common practice for accounts to continue in the principle's name after their death. The account that raises questions concerning Curtis's associations, is the joint account held with Sir John Carter and Sir John Godwin, both of whom were very prominent in Portsmouth society. Both had served as Mayors of Portsmouth during the period 1767 to 1804. In fact, these two men monopolised this office through the influence they held within the Portsmouth Corporation or as it was more popularly known The Carter Group (this was a small select group whose members belonged to the Corporation). 16 Due to this dubious hold over Portsmouth society, both Carter and Godwin have more recently attained suspicious reputations, mainly confirmed through their interest in local business. One of their main associates was local solicitor and shipping broker Thomas Andrews Minchin, proprietor of the Portsea Island Water Works 17 and Sir Roger Curtis's personal Attorney. 18 These three men established the Portsmouth, Portsea and Hampshire Bank, which after a string of changes amongst its directors went into liquidation on 10 November 1818. Added to these failed interests was the open hostility shown by Godwin and Carter to the Admiralty during the 1770s and 1780s over the Admiralty control within the town's local business. 19 This hostility was displayed through the Carter Group who campaigned for changes in Admiralty control. Why did Sir Roger open an account with these men in February 1794 after their avowed hostility towards the navy? More importantly, what was the purpose of an account which lasted for sixteen years, where no entries or withdrawals were made and where the opening entry was deposited by George Carter and not any of the named account holders? Was money being concealed through a third party? All three account holders were men of influence locally, and as such, they would have socialised within the same circles. Moreover, it is possible the Minchin was introduced to Curtis by Carter and Godwin, explaining how that association was formed. However, this is by no means enough to explain the reasons for opening this account. Unfortunately, no material survives to answer this, perhaps because this account was something less than above board? Why Curtis associated with men so hostile towards the Navy, is easier to answer. It is firstly doubtful as to whether this hostility extended to individuals and the friendship that arose was separate from the navy, secondly it is possible that in Curtis, Carter and Godwin saw a 'man on the inside' and through using Curtis had direct access to the Admiralty. Also in the interests of Curtis's move up the social ladder of local society, it would have been in his interests to befriend and be seen with men of local prominence, thus using friendship for his advancement.

Admiral Curtis was very astute when it came to planning the financial futures for his immediate family. He made more than adequate provision for them in his Will, setting up trust funds and leaving immediate lump sums upon his death. The conditions of his Will stipulated that one month after his death his wife and children should receive £500, following which each of them should receive £400 annually for as long as the estate provides. On his wife's death, Lucius and his wife were to receive £5,000. Upon the marriage of his daughter she was to receive £5,000, this was to be given to her as and when the executors see fit. For his grandchildren and any future grandchildren, a further trust fund was set up for them to inherit at the age of twenty one. The money for these funds came from the dividends of his Stock held with the Bank of England and from the rent money acquired from the leasing of his properties. 20 It is unclear as to whether this would have funded all of the trust funds, but when referring to the family tree on page 30, it becomes apparent that three of his grandchildren did not live until they were twenty one and his wife Sarah, only survived for five months after Admiral Curtis's death, passing away on 10 April 1817 at her seat in Gatcombe, aged sixty five. In this respect the financial demands placed upon the fund would have been eased.

Yet the conditions as listed above were his original wishes as expressed in 1811. This date invites questions, as to why he should draw up his Will as late as 1811, especially as the nature of his work would have demanded provision to be made. Perhaps 1811 was a further alteration to an undiscovered previous Will? When subsequent codicils on 27 July, 7 September and 12 November 1816 were added interesting changes were shown concerning the altered nature of family relationships. The principle alteration was the revoking of all previous provision for his daughter Jane. On 7 September 1816 he wrote Jane out if his Will and only commented that any inheritance for her would come from her mother's estate. 21 What motivated this action?

The answer to this lay in the original Will and in the addition made on 7 September. In the original Will be clearly indicated that Jane was unmarried. By 7 September the Will made reference to a grandchild, the daughter of Jane Curtis, though no reference is made to any husband. In this lay the reason for her exclusion. For a man of high social standing and one of this country's most senior naval officers, to have a daughter with a fatherless child was a disgrace to the Curtis name. As a consequence, no further literature on the Curtis family mentions Jane. Furthermore, she is not even mentioned on the family memorial plaques within Catherington Church. It was unfortunate that the child's father could not be traced, even after an extensive search of the local Bastardy bonds register listing those absent fathers who are made to pay for the child by providing a bond, there was still no success. This is because if it turned out to be a colleague or a rival of Admiral Curtis, then this would have brought further shame upon a man by all accounts was a very traditional and proud man. As a result of this exclusion, Lucius Curtis has his trust fund raised to £600 per annum and a new fund was set up for Sir Roger Curtis's sister Mary Fanstone of £20 per annum, as a gesture rather than as a supporting income, as Curtis no doubt considered her financial position as stable following her marriage. 22 Further clues were given in his Will to the nature of Curtis's friendship with Lord Howe. When Sir Roger Curtis divided up his estate, he spoke of a gold chronometer that belonged to Howe that was given to Curtis by Howe's widow. He also mentioned the Rysdale donated to him by the late Lord and Lady Howe. Finally, he alluded to his Gold Chain and Medal presented to him by Lord Howe and George III for his services on the Glorious First of June 1794. 23 For all three articles, so closely associated with Howe, Sir Roger Curtis made it clear that none were to be sold. Rather should they be kept in the family for generations to come. 24 This is a clear indication of the respect and friendship between these two men and stands as a fitting conclusion to their entwined careers together.

Two days after his final entry to the Will, Sir Roger Curtis died aged seventy one. 25 His funeral took place eleven days later and the reporting of it in the Hampshire Telegraph for 25 November 1816 best sums up the mood of the time and the respect for Curtis that this area held for him:

Yesterday the remains of that distinguished and highly esteemed character, Adm. Sir Roger Curtis Bart and GCB were conveyed from his seat, Gatcombe, to Catherington and interned in the family vault at that church. The pall was borne by Admirals Sirs Edward Thorbrough, Sir George Murray, Halkett and Walter Otway, the Hon. Sir George Grey and Sir Archibald Dickson, Sir Lucius Curtis, Bart, Chief Mourner - Capts Holles, C Dashwood, Roger R Hall, J S Hulbert Esq (his late Secretary), T A Minchin and Ely Cooke Esqrs (Executors) and Moses Greetham Esq., followed the mortal remains of the ornament to his country, as mourners. The carriages of Lord Keith, Sir George Grey, Sir Edw. Thornbrough Adm. Halkett, J Williams Esq and H Minchin, closed the mournful scene. The solemn service was performed in the most pathetic strains by the Rev. J Davies of Catherington Church.

It was Admiral Curtis's last wish that he should be buried as privately as possible, under the chancel of Catherington Church. Further to this request was his instruction that a small mural monument was to be erected, for which he had transcribed the form of a brief inscription. 27 See Appendix No. In this description by the *Hampshire Telegraph* there were many names of those who he had served with at Gibraltar and on the Glorious First of June 1794; such as Sir George Murray, Sir George Grey and Sir Archibald Dickson. Another name in this list of particular note was J S Hulbert, Curtis's Secretary. John Spice Hulbert (born April 1778) was a Port Secretary at Portsmouth for twenty years, serving many of its Commander-in-Chief's of whom included Sir Roger Curtis. However, before entering the civil side of the navy, Hulbert was a sailor beginning his career on board the *Temendous* (74) with the rank of Midshipman. It was whilst holding this rank that Hulbert was posted as Midshipman to the *Victory* under the command of Lord Howe, with Curtis as its Flag Captain. Together these three men served on the *Victory* during the famous Glorious First of June 1794, from which a friendship was struck. Hulbert went on to serve on board the *Rattlesnake* in the Cape, at the same time as Curtis was stationed there as Commander-in-Chief. 28 From this close association it became apparent that Hulbert was much more than Curtis's Port Secretary and their friendship was well established well before serving together in Portsmouth from 1809. Following his funeral, Admiral Curtis's estate was to be divided up as per codicils drafted on 12 November 1816. This task was entrusted to his executors for which service they received £200 per annum from the estate. 29 The administration of his estate continued long after 1816, indeed rents were still collected under Admiral Curtis's name up until 1841, the year of Lucius's wife's death, from there his estate is n longer mentioned. This though does not mean that was the end of the administration of his estate.

Conclusion

Throughout the previous chapters a picture has slowly been assembled of Sir Roger Curtis's character that includes his career, family and lifestyle. In so doing, this work has attempted to examine one of this country's most successful, but least written about Admirals. Admiral Curtis came from a well established prosperous background and even though his father had envisaged him following in his footsteps as a gentlemen farmer, this did not stop Curtis in his desire to go to sea. During his naval career his name was linked with many famous battles and many famous men, such as Lord Howe and Earl St Vincent. Owing mainly to these associations, Curtis moved swiftly through the ranks establishing a well respected reputation. This reputation changed the Curtis name from a farming one to a naval one. By the time his two sons, Roger and Lucius, entered the service the Curtis name was well established in the Navy and they went on to strengthen these ties still further. (Thus by the time Lucius's two seafaring sons signed up, the farming association with the family name, which his father had been hoping to preserve had been snapped). This study has mapped his rise from farmer's son to naval hero and attempted to highlight some of the background of Curtis. The experience moulded a character which was one of a fair man, yet forceful in his convictions as a senior naval officer. He distinguished himself on many occasions, proving his worth. His time as Commander-in-Chief, Portsmouth, reflected that of an able administrator and successful diplomat. This was aided by a useful succession of patronage and to this end he attained only the most senior officers as his patrons. Using these friendships, Curtis's successes at sea were well rewarded on land. This, though, should not be viewed as unusual; patronage was a common practice. In Curtis's case, however, his patrons were the most senior in the Navy. This led to jealousy and dislike of Admiral Curtis from other officers, such as Collingwood, who simply saw Curtis as a dog obeying his master.

Outside of his official capacity, Curtis gave the impression of running a successful, stable and much loved family. Along with his finances, which reflected those of a prosperous man, his image was that of a leading figure in Portsmouth society. Yet as with his family, questions were raised concerning this public image. One interesting question concerned his omission from the ranks of the local Literary and Philosophical Society, often considered desirable to those men wishing to obtain and secure their influence and position within the town. Closer to home, the exclusion of his daughter, Jane, from his estate split the family. This revealed a man so concerned with his own image and that of traditionalism, that it lost him his daughter and granddaughter. When this was combined with the tragic loss of his eldest son, Roger, which resulted in a lengthy sick leave, not physical but mental for Curtis, from his duties at Portsmouth, it reveals a Curtis household which was anything but stable.

Stability in Curtis's career also seemed to have been lacking. His close associations and his, on occasions, devious methods employed to secure patronage, for example, the Collingwood letter, reflected a man insecure in his own position as a senior Naval Officer.

The investigation into his bank accounts also cast shadows over his character. His associations and joint account with Godwin and Carter and friendship with Minchin, merit further consideration. So too does his considerable balance in his personal account with many large deposits.

However, this was not the character of a man as portrayed in print. That image was perhaps best summed up in the *Naval Chronicle* for 1808, which a picture was delineated of a lighthearted, caring, generous naval officer:

Having received orders while in London to take command of a squadron at Portsmouth, the Admiral travelled , for dispatch, without servants, plainly dressed, in a mail coach. As it frequently happens in this sort of conveyance, the passengers were unknown to each other and Sir Roger found himself in company with a young man, who proved, by his uniform, to be a mate on one of the East Indiamen then lying at the Motherbank. When they had proceeded within a few miles of Petersfield, the young officer pulled out some bread and cheese from a bundle and invited his fellow travellers to eat. During their repast he entertained them with sea phrases, which induced the Admiral jocosely to ask him many simple questions relating to nautical tactics; among others, he demanded how sailors could see at night and whether they were not compelled to tie the ship to a post or tree until morning? The mate was not backward in bestowing a few hearty don't knows upon the ignorance and lubberly lingo of the Admiral, who laughed heartily at the joke; and he not only bore the rough observation of the sailor with good humour, but the contemptuous grins of his fellow passengers. On their arrival at Portsmouth, the Admiral shook hands with the mate and went on board his ship. The same day Sir Roger came on shore in his broad gold laced hat and uniform; he was attended by several of his bargemen and while walking up Point-street, he met his late fellow-passenger, the mate of the Indiaman. Before the latter could recover from his surprise, Sir Roger accosted him with, 'What cheer, messmate; you see I am not the lubber you took me for; but come, as I breakfasted out of your locker this morning, you shall splice the main-brace with me this evening; then you may square your yards and run before the wind to the Motherbank'. The mate, with astonishment, apologised and well he was able, for the liberty he had taken with the Admiral, who soon released him from his embarrassment and advised him, over a bottle, never to be decoyed in future by false colours, but to look sharply at the mould and trim of every vessel he met, before he suffered her to surprise him.

References

Introduction

1:    D.N.B. Vol IV p348

Chapter One

1:    *NC*, Vol VI, (July-Dec) 1801 p1

2:    J Ralfe, *A Naval Biography of Great Britain*, (2 Vols) Vol 2 p32

3:    *NC*, Vol VI, (July-Dec) 1801 p216

4:    *GM*, (June) 1791 p57

5:    *NC*, Vol VI (July-Dec) 1801 p261

6:    J Ralfe - *A Naval Biography of Great Britain* (2 Vols) Vol 2 p32

7:    *D.N.B.* Vol IV p348

8:    ibid p348

9:    *D.N.B.* Vol X p95

10:   *NC*, Vol VI (July-Dec) 1801 p262

11:   J Ralfe - *A Naval Biography of Great Britain* (2 Vols) Vol 2 p33

42

12:    ibid p33

13:    *NC*, Vol VI (July-Dec) 1801 p262

14:    J Ralfe - *A Naval Biography of Great Britain* (2 Vols) Vol 2

15:    *Dictionary of Nineteenth Century Personages* (nd) p282

16:    *NC*, Vol VI (July-Dec) 1801 p268

17:    ibid pp261-264

18:    ibid pp281-284

19:    ibid p170

20:    ibid p272

21:    J Ralfe - *A Naval Biography of Great Britain* (2 Vols) Vol 2
       p41

22:    *The Spencer Papers 1794-1801, NRS* Vol XLVI p180

23:    *NC*, Vol VI (July-Dec) 1801 p272

24:    ibid p273

25:    W Clowes; *The Royal Navy, A History* (7 Vols 1797-1903 Vol
       V 1803-1815 p255

26:    *The Private Correspondence of Admiral Lord Collingwood,
       NRS* (MNCMLVII) p50

27:    Dr Alexander Carlyle to Collingwood, 9 July 1794, ibid p51

28:    G Murray, *Life of Collingwood* (1936) p45

29:    After the Battle of Trafalgar, Curtis sent a personal letter
       congratulation to Collingwood. *The Private Correspondence
       of Admiral Lord Collingwood, NRS* (MCMLVII p196

30: G Murray, *Life of Collingwood* (1936) p45

31: *Selections from the Correspondence of Admiral John Markham* (NRS 1904) p203

32: *The Spencer Papers 1794-1801, NRS* Vol XLVI p236

33: ibid p191

34: *D.N.B.* Vol X p36. It was not the gout that killed him, but the electricity

35: *D.N.B.* Vol IV p349

Chapter Two

1: *A Naval Encyclopaedia by officers and others of recognised authority in the branches treated by them* (2 Vols) Vol 1 (Detroit) p151

2: M Lewis, *The Navy of Britain* (1949) p81

3: *A Naval Encyclopaedia by officers and others of recognised authority in the branches treated by them* (2 Vols) Vol 1 (Detroit) p152

4: W B Gurney - *The Minutes of the Court Martial of James Lord Gambier* (Portsmouth 1809) p12

5: Jerdan - National Portrait Gallery of Personages in the Nineteenth Century (1830-1834) p312

6: *D.N.B.* Vol VII p834
7: Sir Roger Curtis beat Lord Keith to the post of Commander-in-Chief of Portsmouth

8: *D.N.B* Vol IV p624

9:      ibid p621

10:     Fire Ships - Burning your own vessel and letting it drift into
        the enemy: P Kemp (ed) *Oxford Companion to Ships and the
        Sea* (1976) p305

11:     *D.N.B.* Vol VII p835

12:     *D.N.B.* Vol IV p624

13:     ibid p624

14:     ibid p624

15:     idib p624

16:     W B Gurney - *The Minutes of the Court Martial of James
        Lord Gambier* (Portsmouth 1809) p98

17:     *The Times* 26 July 1809

18:     W B Gurney - *C M Minutes* (Portsmouth 1809) p122

19:     ibid p123

20:     *D.N.B.* Vol IV p625

21:     W B Gurney - *C M Minutes* (Portsmouth 1809) p3

22:     ibid p3

23:     ibid p224

24:     ibid p4
25:     ibid p229

26:     ibid p231

27:     ibid p232

28:   *D.N.B.* Vol IV p625

29:   Admiral Markham to Sir Roger Curtis 10 June 1803, Sir C
      Markham (ed) *Selections from the Correspondence of Admiral
      John Markham* NRS (1904) p418

30:   Sir H Vessy-Hamilton - *Recollections of James A Gardner,
      Commander RN* NRS (1846) p61

31:   ibid p61

32:   J Ralfe - *A Naval Biography of Great Britain* (2 Vols) Vol 2
      p44

Chapter Three

1:    A R F Hynes - The Story of Gatcombe House and Hilsea
      Barracks in the *The R.A.O.C.* Gazette 1949 p342

2:    W G Gates - *Portsmouth in the Past* (nd) p44

3:    *Hampshire Telegraph* 3 June 1833

4:    *NC*, Vol VIII (July-Dec) 1982 p88

5:    Sir C Markham (ed) *Selections from the Correspondence of
      Admiral John Markham* NRS, MCMI p418

6:    W O'Byrne - *A Naval Biographical Dictionary* 1849 p254

7:    S Shuttleworth - *Farms and Market Gardens on Portsea
      Island* 1779-1880 P.P. 12, 1971 p6
8:    *VCH*, Vol IV pp393-395

9:    J F R Hope - *A History of Hunting in Hampshire* 1950 p175

10:   *VCH*, Vol V p68

11:     Unfortunately they do not possess records until after 1830, but
        according to Christopher Purchase, Director, were regular
        suppliers to the Navy and those senior officers within it.

12:     S Shuttleworth - *Farms and Market Gardens on Portsea
        Island* 1770-1880 P.P. 12, 1971 p6

13:     Jacomb Van Ruisdael (Rysdale) (1628-1682). Dutch landscape
        Artist from Amsterdam. Popular in the Eighteenth Century
        with the upper classes and Armed Forces, though not with the
        Landed Gentry: The Oxford Companion to Art (Oxford 1991)

14:     Bank of England Account Folio 10000-10638, a/c
        27/1625/9/23 p10486

15:     Bank of England Account Folio 10000-11095, a/c
        27/1577/9/18 p10037

16:     A Geddes - *Portsmouth during the French Wars* 1770-1800,
        P.P. 9, 1970 p13

17:     M Hallet - *Portsmouth Water Supply* 1800-1860, P.P. 12,
        1971 p17

18:     Originally operating as Minchin and Compigne, Gosport, but
        dissolved on 3 December 1808. *Hampshire Telegraph* 8
        September 1816

19:     A Geddes - *Portsmouth during the French Wars* 1770-1800,
        P.P. 9 1970 p11

20:     The Last Will and Testament of Sir Roger Curtis, December
        1816 , Prob 12/205, Film 1586, No 610
21:     ibid

22:     ibid

23:     This was the first recognised Naval Medal. M Lewis
        Spithead, passim

24: The Last Will and Testament of Sir Roger Curtis, December 1816, Prob 12/205, Film 1586, No 610

25: Although he described himself as always approaching seventy *NC*, Vol XXXVII (Jan-June) 1817 p103

26: *Hampshire Telegraph* 25 November 1816

27: *NC*, Vol XXXVII (Jan-June) 1817 p103

28: Taken from *An account of J S Hulbert* by his son P.C.R.O. 626A/1/5/1/7

29: Bank of England Account Folio 10000-11095 a/c 27/1577/9/18 p10037

Conclusion

1: *NC*, Vol XX (1808) pp199-200

Appendix A

Sir Roger Curtis's Naval Career

Rank	Month	Year
Midshipman	?	1762
Lieutenant	19 January	1771
Commander	11 July	1776
Captain	30 April	1777
Rear Admiral of the Blue	4 July	1794
Rear Admiral of the Red	1 June	1795
Vice Admiral of the White	14 February	1799
Vice Admiral of the Red	1 January	1801
Admiral of the Blue	23 April	1804
Admiral of the White	9 November	1805
Admiral of the Red	31 July	1810

(Colours indicate different squadrons with the fleet)

Commander-in-Chief	From	Until
The Cape of Good Hope	1799	1804
Portsmouth	1809	1815

Source: *The Commissioned Sea Officers of the Royal Navy
1660-1815 (2 Vols) Vol 1 (A-F) p224*

Appendix B
British and French line of battle on 1 June 1794

BRITISH.   FRENCH.

Ships.	Guns.	Commanders.	Killed.	Wounded.	Ships.	Guns.	Commanders.
					Trajan . . .	74	Capt. Dumoutier.
Cæsar . . .	80	Capt. Anthony James Pye Molloy.	18	71	Eole . . .	74	„ Bertrand Keranguen.[2]
Bellerophon .	74	{ Rear-Admiral Thomas Pasley (W).[1] Capt. William Johnstone Hope.[1]	4	27	America[3] . .	74	{ „ Louis L'Héritier. „ Morel.
					Téméraire . .	74	
Leviathan .	74	„ Lord Hugh Seymour.[1]	10	33	Terrible . .	110	{ Rear-Admiral François-Joseph Bouvet. Capt. Julien Le Ray.
Russell . . .	74	{ „ John Willett Payne.[1]	8	26	Impétueux[3] .	74	„ Douville.
					Mucius . .	74	„ Larreguy.
Royal Sovereign	100	{ Vice-Admiral Thomas Graves (2) (R).[1] Capt. Henry Nicholls.[1]	14	44	Tourville . .	74	„ Langlois.
					Gasparin . .	74	„ Tardy.
Marlborough .	74	{ „ Hon. George Cranfield Berkeley.[1]	29	90	Convention .	74	„ Joseph Allary.
					Trente - et - un Mai . . }	74	{ „ Honoré Ganteaume.
Defence . . .	74	„ James Gambier (2).[1]	18	39	Tyrannicide .	74	„ d'Ordelin.
					Juste[3] . . .	80	„ Blavet.
Impregnable .	98	{ Rear-Admiral Benjamin Caldwell (W). Capt. George Blagden Westcott.	7	21	Montagne . .	120	{ Rear-Admiral Louis Thomas Villaret-Joyeuse. Capt. Bazire.[2]
Tremendous .	74	„ James Pigott.	3	8	Jacobin . .	80	„ Gassin.
Barfleur . .	98	{ Rear-Admiral George Bowyer (W).[1] Capt. Cuthbert Collingwood.	9	25	Achille[3] . .	74	{ „ G. J. N. de La Villegris.
					Vengeur du Peuple[4] . }	74	{ „ Jean François Renaudin.
Invincible .	74	{ „ Hon. Thomas Pakenham.[1]	14	31	Patriote . .	74	„ Lucadou.
Culloden . .	74	„ Isaac Schomberg.	2	5	Northumberland[3] . }	74	{ „ François Etienne.
Gibraltar . .	80	„ Thomas Mackenzie.	2	12	Entreprenant .	74	„ Le Franeq.
					Jemmapes[5] .	74	„ Desmartis.
Queen Charlotte	100	{ Admiral Earl Howe (Union).[1] Capt. Sir Roger Curtis, Kt. (1st)[1] „ Sir Andrew Snape Douglas, Kt.[1]	14	29	Neptune . .	74	„ Tiphaigne.
					Pelletier . .	74	„ Berrade.
Brunswick .	74	„ John Harvey.[1]	44	114	Républicain .	110	{ Rear-Admiral Joseph Marie Nielly. Capt. Pierre Jacques Longer.
Valiant . .	74	„ Thomas Pringle.[1]	2	9			
Orion . . .	74	{ „ John Thomas Duckworth.[1]	5	24	Sans Pareil[3] .	80	{ „ Jean François Courand.
Queen . . .	98	{ Rear-Admiral Alan Gardner (W).[1] Capt. John Hutt.[2]	36	67	Scipion . .	80	„ Huguet.
Ramillies . .	74	„ Henry Harvey.	2	7	Précieuse, 36 .		
Alfred . .	74	„ John Bazely (1).	..	8	Naïade . .		
Montagu . .	74	„ James Montagu.[2]	4	13	Proserpine, 40 .		
					Tamise, 32 . }	..	{ „ J. M. A. L'Hermite.
Royal George	100	{ Vice-Admiral Sir Alexander Arthur Hood, K.B.(R).[1] Capt. William Domett.[1]	20	72	Papillon . .		
Majestic . .	74	„ Charles Cotton.	3	18	Galatée, 36 .		
Glory . .	98	{ „ John Elphinstone (2).[1]	13	39	Gentille, 36 .		
Thunderer .	74	„ Albemarle Bertie.					

And three or four small craft.

Ships.		Commanders.	Killed.	Wounded.
Phaeton, 38 .	..	„ William Bentinck.	3	4
Latona, 38 .	..	{ „ Edward Thornbrough.		
Niger, 32 .	..	{ „ Hon. Arthur Kaye Legge.		
Southampton, 32 . }	..	„ Hon. Robert Forbes.		
Venus, 32 .	..	„ William Brown (1).		
Aquilon, 32 .	..	{ „ Hon. Robert Stopford.		
Pegasus, 28 .	..	„ Robert Barlow.		
		Total . .	290	858

[1] Received medals, as having particularly signalised themselves. Capt. William Parker, of the *Audacious*, also received a medal for his conduct on May 28th, and Capt. Cuthbert Collingwood, of the *Barfleur*, after protest, received one at a later period.
[2] Killed, or mortally wounded.
[3] Struck and made prize of.
[4] Struck and foundered.
[5] Struck, but retaken by the French.

Source: W Clowes; The Royal Navy - A History (7 Volumes 1897-1903), Vol IV p226

Appendix C

Dillon's account of 25 June 1794

25 June 1794, Portsmouth

Sir William Dillon, then a Midshipman, described George III's visit to Portsmouth:

> They went on board the *Queen Charlotte*. To the noble and gallant Admiral Lord Howe, His Majesty presented a diamond hilted sword of the value of 3,000 guineas, also a gold chain to be worn round the neck. The Royal Party dined that day on board with his Lordship. It was whispered on that occasions that the King intended investing the peer with the Order of the Garter. However, rumours in circulation led me to believe that the ministers' political prejudices restrained the Royal will. After dinner the Royal Party returned on shore. They were saluted and cheered by the whole Fleet, both coming and going.
>
> The two next Senior Admirals, Graves and Hood, were created Irish peers: the four Rear-Admirals, baronets. All the Flag Officers received gold chains similar to that given to Lord Howe and the Captains received medals - at least a certain number of them. Pensions were settled on all that were wounded. All the Senior Lieutenants of the ships of the Line that were in action received the rank of Commander. The Master of the *Queen Charlotte*, Mr Bowen, was made a Lieutenant and later, became a Commissioner and a Rear-Admiral - a rare feat in those days for a mere Warrant Officer.

After this, His Majesty remained for several days, holding a series of levees and doing all that he could to enhance the Navy's reputation. But he did not hold a formal Review, leading the Fleet in his own yacht. In fact, he probably did not possess a yacht at that time or, at any rate, did not have one with him at Portsmouth.

Source: M Lewis, *Spithead - An Informal History* (1972)
pp164-165

NB - When comparing this with the original script in *Dillon's Narrative* ed. by M Lewis for the *NRS* (1953), it is apparent that the text above is an edited version of a lengthy description, which included an account of officers angry at their omission from the medal list, protesting to Howe and attempting to make their feelings known for the Kings visit. pp150-154.

Appendix D

Sir Roger Curtis to Admiral John Markham 10 June 1803 (son died 12 July 1802)

64 Jermyn Street, 10 June 6pm

My dear Sir, I am at length arrived in London and should have left Portsmouth the day after I struck my flag, but Lady Curtis was so dangerously ill I could not leave her. She has not, nor will ever, recover from the grief which she has been afflicted by the loss of my son. She has told me much of your goodness towards her and is very grateful for it, and so am I.

I particularly request you will do me the favour to let me know this evening by a short note, at what time tomorrow morning it will be the most likely for me to have the honour of paying my respects to Lord St Vincent, which I wish to do so as soon as may be, that I may go into dock under the care of Sir James Earle, with a view to be made without delay fit for service.

I am with great esteem, my dear Sir,

Most faithfully yours,
ROGER CURTIS

Captain Markham, &c.,&c.,&c..

Source: Sir C Markham (ed) - *Selections from the correspondence of Admiral John Markham NRS* (1904) p418

Appendix E

These are the inscriptions to members of the Curtis family recorded in
Catherington Church, where the family vault is located.

The inscriptions are positioned to the left and right of the altar.

Left of the Altar:

Roger Curtis Esq.
Captain in the Royal Navy
Died on 12 July 1802, Aged 22 years
Possessing eminent Abilities in his Profession.
He was of the most admiral Disposition and Manners
and an Ornament of Society. His much afflicted Parents,
Vice Admiral SIR ROGER CURTIS, BART and LADY CURTIS,
with the deepest Sorrow for his untimely Death
erect this Tablet to
HIS MEMORY.

To the memory of
Roger William Curtis Esq.
Son of Admiral Sir Lucius and Lady Curtis
Died at the island of Trinidad, West Indies
on 23 September 1859 aged 42 years
Also of
Lucius Irwin, son of the above Roger William Curtis,
who died at East Cosham in the county of Hampshire
on 25 January 1860 aged 3 years and 7 months.

To the memory of
Eliza Burtler Curtis
Relickt of
Roger William Curtis Esq.
who died at Brighton on 4 November 1878 aged 47 years.
To the memory of

Roger Lucius Curtis Lieut RN
Son of Sir Lucius and Lady Curtis
who died at Bahia, South America
while on command of
H M Steam Vessel _____
The 6 October _____
Aged _____ years.

Roger Curtis Commander RN
Son of the above
Died 26 December 1845 aged 44 years.

Right of the Altar: (in a Gothic style)

Sacred
To the Memory of
Sir Lucius Curtis, BART, KCB
Admiral of the Fleet
Son of Admiral
Sir Roger Curtis and Lady Curtis
Born AD 1786
Died at East Cosham, AD 1869
Aged 83 years.

This Tablet
is erected to the Memory of
Mary Figg Curtis
Wife of Rear Admiral Sir Lucius Curtis, Bart, CB
who died deeply lamented by her bereaved family
and sincerely regretted by her friends
30 May aged 51 years
also Howe
who died 30 January 1824
Aged 3 years and 7 months
George Henville
who died 6 February 1824
Aged 2 years 5 months

Roger Frederick
who died 14 July 1835
Aged 16 years
Sons of Rear Admiral and Sir Lucius and Lady Curtis.

To the Memory of
Sir Roger Curtis, Knight and Baronet
Knight Grand Cross of the most Honourable
Military Order of the Bath
and Admiral of the Red
who died on 14 November 1816
in the 71st year of his age
Also of Dame Sarah Curtis
who died the 10 April 1817
in the 65th year of her age.

This first part of this inscription for Sir Roger Curtis was written by him in the last year of his life.

Source: All Saints Church, Catherington, MIs

Bibliography

**Place of Publication is London
Unless otherwise stated**

Manuscript Sources:

Bank of England
Account - Sir Roger Curtis (personal)
1788-1792, folio 10000-11095 number 8, a/c
27/1577/9/18 p10037

Account - Sir Roger Curtis, John Carter, John Godwin
(joint) 1792-1798, folio 10000-10638 number 9, a/c
27/1625/9/23 p10486

Boston Public Library USA
Letters from Sir Roger Curtis 1809-15

Brenhurst Library, South Africa
Journal 1799-1802 including Records of the Cape Colony
(968.704 THE)

British Library
Letters and Orders of Sir Thomas Cochrane, 10th Earl
November 1807 - July 1849 (27 Vols) 12-15 MSS 2577-2604
National Library of Scotland: SRO GD 233/65/11

Huntington Library USA
Letters from Lord Howe (408)
256-299

National Maritime Museum

60

NRA 30121 Mus (JOD/157) Journal of the Embassy to
Morocco 1793

Public Record Office
Prob 12/165, Film 1205, number 273 - The Last Will and
Testament of Roger Curtis, Wilts, June 1791

Prob 12/205, Film 1586, number 610 - The Last Will and
Testament of Sir Roger Curtis, December 1816

Primary Printed Sources
W B Gurney, Minutes of a Court Martial in the trial of
James Lord Gambier: on board His Majesty's Ship *Gladiator*
Portsmouth 1809

Publications of the Navy Records Society
Sir Clements Markham (ed) *Selections from the Correspondence
of Admiral John Markham* 1904

Admiral Sir Vessey-Hamilton (ed) *Recollections of James
Anthony Gardner,* Commander RN, Vol XXXI (1906)

Anon *Letters of Admiral of the Fleet The Earl St Vincent*
1801-1804 (1922)

J Corbett, *The Spencer Papers* (2Vols 1946-8)

Rear Admiral H Richmond, ibid, Vol IV (1948)

Anon *The Keith Papers*, Vol I (1927) and II (1950)

M Lewis (ed) *Dillon's Narrative* (1953)

Anon *The Private Correspondence of Admiral Lord Collingwood*
(1957)

Directories, Magazines and Newspapers

Directories
Universal British Directory, Gosport and Portsmouth entried 1798

Magazines
The Annual Register for 1817

Gentleman's Magazine Vol LXXXVII (1817)

Naval Chronicle Vols 1-XXXVII 1799-1817

Newspapers
Hampshire Chronicle 1802-1869

Hampshire Telegraph 1802-1869

Times July-August 1809

Secondary Sources
Anon   *Concise Catalogue of Oil Paintings in the National Maritime Museum* (Suffolk 1988)

Anon   *Catalogue of Portraits and Prints* (National Maritime Museum nd)

Anon   *A New Biographical Dictionary of ... Contemporary* (sic) *Public Characters* (6 Vols 1825)

Anon   *The Commissioned Sea Officers of the Royal Navy, 1660-1815* (4 Vols, 1, 1954)

Anon   *A Naval Encyclopaedia* by Officers and others of recognised authority in the branches treated by them (USA 1971)

Sir S E Brydges, *A Biography, Peerage of the Empire of Great Britain* (4 Vol 1808-1817) 1832 edn)

Sir B Burke, A Genalogical and Heraldic Dictionary of the Gentry of Great Britain and Northern Ireland (1863)

W O'Byrne, *A Naval Biographical Dictionary* (1849)

G Callender, *Sea Kings of Britain* (Keppel to Nelson) (1930)

A J Camp, *An Index to the Wills proved in the Prerogative Court of Canterbury* 1750-1800 Vol III 1984

V Bonham-Carter, *In a Liberal Tradition, A Social Biography 1700-1950* (1960)

W L Clowes, *The Royal Navy, A History* (7 Vols 1897-1903)

Dictionary of National Biography: Vols IV, VI, VII, VIII, X, XI, XIII, XXI, (1911)

W Gates, *Portsmouth Through the Centuries* (nd)

W Gates, *Portsmouth in the Past* (Portsmouth 1972)

M Hallett, *Portsmouth Water Supply 1800-1860.* Portsmouth Paper 12 May 1971 (Portsmouth)

Brig-Gen J F R Hope, *A History of Hunting in Hampshire* (Winchester 1950)

W James, *The Naval History of Great Britain* (5 Vols 1886)

J Delafons, *Naval Court Martials* (1805)
D Hannay, *Naval Court Martial* (Cambridge 1914)

A Geddes, *Portsmouth during the French Wars 1770-1800*, Portsmouth Paper 9 March 1970 (Portsmouth)

W Jerdan, *National Portrait Gallery ... personages of the Nineteenth Century* (5 Vols 1830-1834)

M Lewis, *England's Sea Officers: The Story of the Naval Profession (1939)*

M Lewis, *The Navy of Great Britain* (1948)

M Lewis, *Spithead* (1972)

G J Marcus, *A Naval History of England: The Age of Nelson* (2 Vols) 1971

Oxford Companion to Art (Oxford University Press 1991)

J Ralfe, *The Naval Biography of Great Britain* (2 Vols 1828)

N A M Rodger, *The Admiralty* (Suffolk 1979)

P Rogers, *Cosham with Widley and Hilsea*, in old picture postcards (Netherlands 1986)

E S Roscoe, *Studies in the History of the Admiralty and Prize Courts* (1932)

S Shuttleworth, *Farms and Market Gardens on Portsea Island 1770-1880, Portsmouth Paper 61 July 1993* (Portsmouth)

D Thomas, *Britannia's Last Sea King* (New York 1978)

W Tute, *A Life of Admiral the Earl of Dundonald* (1965)

Victoria County History: Hampshire Vols II-V, Wiltshire Vols III-VI
T H Ward, Men in the Reign of Queen Victoria (1885)

64

Journal Articles

A C Gutridge, 'Aspects of Naval Prize Agency 1793-1815'
The Mariners Mirror Vol 80, No 1 (February 1994) pp45-53

A Hynes, 'The Story of Gatcombe House and Hilsea Barracks'
The R A O C Gazatte (1949)

Unpublished Typescript Studies

'An Account of J S Hulbert's Life, written by his son'
Portsmouth City Records Office 626 A/1/6/7